WHAT IS GOD'S AREA CODE?

Cartoons for New Children

A Kelly-Duke Book

By

Jack Moore

*With an Afterword for Parents and Teachers
By Andrew M. Greeley*

Sheed and Ward, Inc.
Subsidiary of Universal Press Syndicate

ISBN: 0-8362-0582-0 (paper)
ISBN: 0-8362-0601-0 (hardbound)

Library of Congress Catalog Card Number 74-1545

Hello . . .? Anybody there?

Don't bother me, boy, I'm making a long distance call.

Who are you calling?

God

Duke, Duke, Duke ...

You can't get God on the phone!

YOU'RE telling *ME!?*

I can't even get a *DIAL TONE!*

Duke, you don't have to call God on the phone. You can talk to God *any time* by praying.

I know *THAT!* But I want to hear Him when he *ANSWERS!*

Hello, Hello! Is that you, God? This is —
No, No, operator! Not Dial-a-prayer! I want
to talk to God.

No, I don't know the area code.

***NO, I DON'T WANT TO TALK TO YOUR
SUPERVISOR! I WANT TO TALK TO . . .***
Hello, heaven, I'd like to speak with God,
please.

God ... capital G ... O ... D ... tell him it's a friend.

Yes ... What? *WHO?* No, no, I'm not God! I want to *TALK* to God.

I think I got the night shift.

Look, all I want to do is talk to God. He's
what . . . ? Okay, thanks.

God just stepped out of his office.

Out of his office? Where was he?

Washington . . . He got a job as technical
advisor on some ethical problems.

If God had to go out and get a job, it must
be worse in heaven than it is here.

WHAT must be worse?

24

Unemployment ... Angels and aerospace ... I guess they're all taking a beating.

Well, if you can't get God on the phone, what are you going to do?

I'm writing Him a letter.

"Dear Mr. Big" ...?

What else?

Do you mind if I read it?

"Dear Mr. Big:
 If you ever want to see your chickens
again, or your tigers or whales or polar
bears you'll—"

DUKE, THIS IS A RANSOM NOTE!!

I KNOW IT'S A RANSOM NOTE! I WROTE IT!

WHY ARE YOU SENDING GOD A RANSOM NOTE?

'CAUSE I COULDN'T GET HIM ON THE PHONE!

What happens if God doesn't pay the ransom?

I don't even want to think about it.

How much ransom are you asking?

My price is ten dollars ...

in small bills ...

and two parachutes.

40

What are the parachutes for?

In case I have to go pick up the ten dollars.

Are you really going to mail that ransom note to God?

Of course I'm not going to *MAIL IT!*

If I send it through the mail, He'll never get
it! I'm using a messenger service.

But first I've got to make a copy for the devil.

THE DEVIL?

Sure, I might be able to make a better deal with the devil.

God isn't going to like that, Duke.

What? God runs a closed shop? Competition makes the world go around! *IF GOD CAN'T HACK IT HE SHOULD —*

DUKE!!

50

God is going to be very angry with you.

GOD isn't going to know who sent it.

Duke, you don't have to call God on the phone, or write to Him. God is everywhere, he hears everything you say, He even hears your thoughts.

53

What?

I said God even hears your thoughts.

You mean He knows what I'm thinking?

That's right, big fella.

Boy, your puppy is in a lot of trouble.

If God *IS* everywhere, He could be standing right next to me!

He could be in my fur ...

He could be in my ear ...

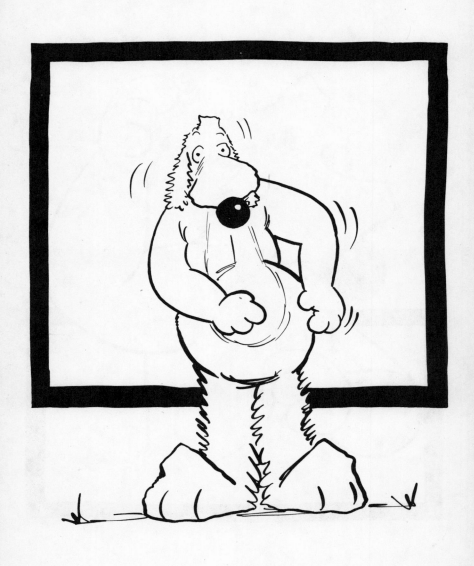

He could be in my pocket or ...

MY POCKET!!

There were two cheeseburgers in here yesterday!

Say boy ... are you *SURE* God can hear my thinking?

Very sure.

GOD'S GOT MY BRAIN BUGGED!

What are you doing?

I'm hiding, dummy! What does it look like
I'm doing?

Duke, you can't hide from God.

Then I'll wear a disguise ... I'll change my name ... I'll ...

It won't work, Duke.

The American Civil Liberties Union will put a stop to *THIS!*

Put a stop to what?

GOD BUGGED MY MIND WITHOUT A COURT ORDER!

Duke, if you send that ransom note to God,
I don't want to be around when the
lightning strikes.

There isn't a cloud in the —

RUMBLE   RUMBLE

Oh dear.

DON'T DO IT!
DON'T DO IT!
I'LL BE GOOD!

BOY, DID YOU HEAR THE RUMBLE? DID
YOU HEAR IT? GOD REALLY DID HEAR
ME! THERE REALLY IS A GOD! THERE
REALLY IS A GOD!

'Course He's a little mad at me right now,

BUT THERE REALLY IS A GOD! AND HE REALLY CAN HEAR ME!

Well, I hope you've learned your lesson, Duke.

Oh, I have, I *HAVE!*

And I'm going to get in on this religion thing while it's *HOT!*

Oh no!

Under the G ... 29 ... G29

Afterword for Parents and Teachers

By Andrew M. Greeley

KELLY, DUKE AND THE GROUND OF BEING

Me, I'm on the side of Duke.

We did not, to begin with, ask to be thrust into existence. Nor did we ask to be thrust into existence in this particular universe, or in this particular thrust of the cosmic yo-yo. We were not asked whether we approved of our heredity or environment, of our social class, of our ethnic group, of our language or our life style. All of this was thrust upon us without our wishes in the matter being taken into consideration at all. We are stuck with what we've got—like it or not.

So here we are existing in the midst of bafflement. Why do we exist at all? Why does anything exist at all? Is there any plan or purpose in what exists? Is there any plan or purpose in my existence? Is it all a senseless cosmic buzz or, lurking out there somewhere or other—or maybe deep down inside somewhere or other—is there benignity, graciousness, perhaps even passion?

Who's responsible? Beings, take us to your leader. Somebody has to render an account for the universe. Will whoever that somebody is, please stand up and identify himself? We would like to examine, indeed, cross-examine him. He's responsible for a hell of a lot, and the least he can do is provide us with answers as to what he had in mind. And if he has any tape recordings of the conversation that occurred at the heavenly drinking bout which must have preceded the thrusting into existence of our-

91

selves and our world, would he please turn over those tapes lest we have to go to Judge Sirica and get a subpoena.

So, Duke's request is perfectly understandable. If there is a God, and if he's willing to assume responsibility for the mess around us, then he certainly ought to make himself available for a phone conversation. If we can dial the weather, and the time, and a prayer for the day, and advice when we want to commit suicide, surely we ought to be able to dial God, if only to get a tape-recorded message at the other end of the line which would give us a brief summary of what the hell is going on.

We all are really on Duke's side, you know. We may laugh at him, great big oaf of a dog that he is (he reminds me of a St. Bernard I know named Penelope; the earth trembles when Penelope comes lumbering in your direction). We want the Deity who is responsible for the universe to come to terms with us, if not in person, at least through Henry Kissinger, who presumably will be willing to act as a go-between—if the Pope does not feel up to it. What we would like, please, is a detailed description of the divine plan and a precise specification of what is expected from us. Would the Lord God please submit to us a draft of a treaty of nonaggression and cooperation. If he will tell us exactly what he wants and make clear what the rewards will be if we go along with him then at least we'll have a solid basis for negotiation, and since to tell the truth, he holds most of the high cards, we'll be happy to accept his draft with only minor modifications. That is, after all, what poor Duke wants and his request does not seem to be terribly unreasonable. Why won't God play it that way? Or, to put the matter differently, why won't God play it our way? It may not really be necessary for him to have a hot line in his office in the New Jerusalem, but couldn't he at least provide something besides a busy signal when we try to get in touch with him?

Perceive the smugness in Kelly's position. Don't be deceived by that forelock of hair, the hands in the pocket, the casual, cool behavior of an eight-year-old male. Kelly is an existentialist, a kind of Jean Paul Sartre of the lower primary grades. Kelly doesn't need certainty. He is prepared to put up with the world of ambiguity, confusion, conflicting data, and a peekaboo God. Kelly doesn't want, apparently doesn't need, an explanation. The mere fact of existence is enough for him—an attitude that one might expect from an eight-year-old. He does not want to fill in all the details of the divine plan. He does not want a specification of his part in the plan. He apparently does not need a Kissinger to shuttle back and forth in complex negotiations with the Deity. God, says Kelly, is everywhere. That is apparently enough.

So he does not only require God's area code. He must remonstrate with his overgrown puppy when that latter worthy gives vent to our human (and apparently canine also) frustrations over a God who plays hide and seek with the human race that is clearly "It." Where, after all, is He? Lurking out behind Alphis and Tauri, or maybe just around the drugstore corner? Out in some quadrant of the galaxy that even the star ship Enterprise has not explored? Or maybe in the rosebush that's doing its best to be reborn on this cold April day. Duke doesn't know what to make of a God like that, and I understand him. Kelly, unsophisticated eight-year-old existentialist that he is, seems content with a God who at best is a frolicsome Peter Pan and, at worst, a will-o'-the-wisp, always slipping through our fingers.

We can, one supposes, pay our money and take our choice. We can demand a God like Duke wants or we can accept a God like the one Kelly accepts. The only trouble is that Duke—and the rest of us—continue to get the busy signal.

Not so long ago, I made the mistake in public print of temporarily espousing Kelly's position. I admitted that my faith was tentative and hesitant, and argued that no more could any man claim.

I got clobbered by a considerable number of Dukes. How could I be a Catholic priest and admit to anything but absolute certainty. If one was a Christian how could one still be hesitant and tentative? For the Dukes of the world, no lonely moments in which one makes the blind leap of faith, no searing anxieties, no angst, no existential fears. Everything is clear, precise, specific— black and white, no ambiguity, no uncertainty, no gray. For Duke and his breed (incidentally, what breed *is* Duke?) faith is not a certainty leaping from and existing with doubt and anxiety. It's a clear, simple proposition that leaves the cosmos cut and dried.

Well, I learned my lesson, and Kelly, old fella, you can play the game of existential leaps of commitment of the total personality. I'll go along with your buddy, Duke, and René Descartes, and the letter writers, and think it's all clear, simple and easy. What was that phone number again, Duke?

However, if one purports to be a Christian one must go even beyond Kelly's position, or at least make clear that which is implicit in his existentialist nonchalance. For the Christian message—or one should say, the Yahwehist message because it all began on Sinai—is not that we need God's area code but that he has ours. It is not so much that we're trying to get God on the line but that he's frantically trying to phone us. The relationship between God and man is a dialogue all right, but it's one that he initiated, and the fundamental question of human existence is whether we're going to respond to his phone call. The Christian would argue that if Duke got off the line long enough, and sat patiently enough, the phone would ring and there God would be, and he would discover that it was not a new and strange voice but a voice of an old friend he had encountered somewhere before.

The very thrust into existence is the beginning of the dialogue. It is an act of love demanding a response, and all the glories and wonders and surprises of human life are more requests for response. There is always a voice calling if not on the telephone, then from across the river and through the trees, a voice bidding us to come forth. Put the damned telephone down, Duke, and come over on my side of the river. But even though the voice keeps calling, sometimes loudly, sometimes softly, we're never quite sure that we really hear it. Maybe it's our imagination or maybe someone is playing a trick on us or maybe it's simply the wind rustling in the leaves or the water flowing over stones. Besides, it's much safer on this side of the river, and who knows whether there will even be telephones on the other side. Anyway, *what* voice?

If Kelly was the kind of kid who really enjoyed scoring points—which is to say, if he was really as Irish as his name implies—he could really back poor old Duke into a corner. He could warn the ponderous pup that if he continued to fool around the telephone, the voice on the other side of the river might cross the river and might begin pursuing him with unperturbed pace and majestic instance. What would poor Duke do if he discovered that he was being pursued by a hound dog who was quite prepared to chase him down the nights and down the years? One suspects that Duke has had some experience with hound dogs and wouldn't be all that enthusiastic about a heavenly hound chasing him. A God who doesn't seem to be on the other end of the telephone line is one thing; a God who is a hound dog yapping at your heels and chasing you through the swamps and forests, that's something else again.

One suspects that Kelly and Duke are going to be with us for a long time. Existentialist and materialist, they are creatures of our own era. Intellectually I'm on Kelly's side; emotionally, damn it all, I've got to concede Duke's points.

But one suspects this is where Jack Moore is, too, yearning perhaps for his own simple faith of childhood and surely Kelly must be Moore as a little boy or perhaps the little boy who still exists in Moore. Duke responds to the nonchalant, boyish, existentialism with the weary, angry cynicism of the middle years, but Duke is still lovable simply because he's Duke, for beneath all the cynicism there is a raffish little boy in Duke, too. Duke, the ponderous pup, is ancient, as old as sin, but Duke, the comic, proposing to complain to the ACLU about God bugging the universe, is as much a little boy as Kelly. Huckleberry Finn and Tom Sawyer, Penrod and Sam, they are alive and well.

And unless you become like little children you will not enter into the Kingdom of Heaven.